Searchlight BOOKS™

What Are Energy Sources?

Finding Out about

Coal, Oil, and Natural Gas

Matt Doeden

Lerner Publications Company
Minneapolis

Lerner Publications Company
A division of Lerner Publishing Group, Inc.
241 First Avenue North
Minneapolis, MN 55401 USA

For reading levels and more information, look up this title at www.lernerbooks.com.

Library of Congress Cataloging-in-Publication Data

Doeden, Matt.
        Finding out about coal, oil, and natural gas / by Matt Doeden.
            pages   cm — (Searchlight books. What are energy sources?)
        Includes index.
        ISBN 978-1-4677-3654-1 (lib. bdg. : alk. paper)
        ISBN 978-1-4677-4637-3 (eBook)
        1. Coal—Juvenile literature. 2. Petroleum—Juvenile literature. 3. Natural gas—
Juvenile literature. 4. Fossil fuels—Juvenile literature. I. Title.
        TP325.D595 2015
        553.2—dc23   2013041698

Manufactured in the United States of America
1 – BP – 7/15/14

Contents

Chapter 1

COAL, OIL, AND NATURAL GAS

Flip on a light switch. Ride in a car or a truck. Take a trip on a train. Or just turn up the heat in your home. What do all these activities have in common? They require energy.

Riding in a car requires energy. What is another activity that requires energy?

But where does the energy come from? Odds are that it comes from coal, oil, or natural gas. These three fossil fuels have provided the world with most of its energy for hundreds of years.

Train cars such as these carry coal to power plants.

Alternatives to fossil fuels include wind energy. The machines below, called wind turbines, turn energy from wind into electricity.

Alternative energy sources are on the rise. These include solar and wind power. But fossil fuels remain the backbone of the world's energy supply.

What Is a Fossil Fuel?

Most fossil fuels formed around 300 million years ago. This was during a time called the Carboniferous Period. Earth was rich with life at the time. As plants and animals died, many sank beneath swamps or oceans. Eventually they formed a spongy material called peat.

Peat forms when trees and other living things die and break down in wetlands.

The peat pictured here is just like the peat that became fossil fuels over millions of years.

Over millions of years, sand, mud, and rock settled on top of the peat. As the peat sunk lower, it came across high pressures and temperatures. Depending on its location, peat formed from different types of dead plants and animals. It also encountered different pressures and temperatures. Depending on these conditions, the peat eventually formed coal (a solid), oil (a liquid), or natural gas.

Fossil fuels are made mostly of hydrocarbons. Hydrocarbons are energy-rich compounds made of hydrogen and carbon. When fossil fuels burn, the hydrocarbon bonds break. This releases lots of energy. We use this energy to power cars, heat our homes, and make electricity.

The engine in this car burns gasoline and turns it into the energy the car needs to move.

Where Are Fossil Fuels Found?

Most fossil fuels are found underground. They're still buried by all of that rock and dirt. Many deposits of oil and natural gas sit beneath oceans. Or they are in places where oceans once stood. That's because oceans are rich in small plants called algae. These tiny plants made up most of the material that created oil and natural gas.

Oil and natural gas tend to form under water.

The opposite is true for coal. Most coal formed under solid ground rather than under oceans. That's because coal formed mostly from dead trees and plants. So coal deposits are found underneath land where large, swampy forests once stood.

The remains of swampy, forested land helped form coal.

Chapter 2

TURNING FUEL INTO ENERGY

Turning fossil fuels into easily used energy is a long process. Scientists must first find the deposits. The fuels must be collected and refined. Then they're ready to be burned for their energy.

A scientist searches for coal deposits. What is the next step to turn a fossil fuel into usable energy?

Collecting Coal, Oil, and Natural Gas

Each fossil fuel is collected in a slightly different way. Coal is usually mined using two main methods. They are surface mining and underground mining.

Coal mining is hard and dirty work.

Trucks collect coal at a surface mine.

Surface mining is useful when coal is near the surface. Miners dig holes and place explosives into them. The explosives blow the rock and soil off the coal. Then miners collect it.

Underground mining is used when coal deposits are deep. Miners dig tunnels hundreds or even thousands of feet underground. They dig out the coal. Machines called conveyor belts carry it to the surface.

Miners use machines that have special blades to break up the coal.

Oil rigs can be built on land and over water.

Most oil is collected by drilling and pumping. Geologists find an oil deposit. Then a machine called an oil rig drills a hole down to it. Workers place a steel pipe in the hole. At first, pressure causes the oil to spurt out of the pipe. When the pressure drops, pumps bring the oil to the surface. The oil that comes out of the ground is called crude oil.

The process is similar for natural gas. Geologists find deposits. Workers drill down to the gas to create a well. They bring the natural gas to the surface through pipes.

Workers drill pipes into the ground to collect natural gas.

People used to burn off natural gas. Now they sell it as fuel.

Oil and natural gas often form together. So a lot of natural gas comes from the same deposits as oil. They can be collected side by side. Years ago, people burned off the natural gas as a waste product. But they soon learned that it was a valuable fuel.

New Collection Methods

In recent decades, scientists have found new sources of oil and natural gas. Shale is a rock that can be rich with types of oil and natural gas. Miners collect the rock. Then they bake the shale at very high temperatures. This forces the oil out of the rocks. This oil is very similar to crude oil.

Shale is baked at high temperatures to force the oil out.

Another method called hydraulic fracturing, or fracking, has also become popular. Workers drill wells deep underground. Then they pump water, sand, and chemicals into them. These materials cause shale that is deep underground to fracture, or break. This releases oil and gas. Workers pump these fuels to the surface to be collected.

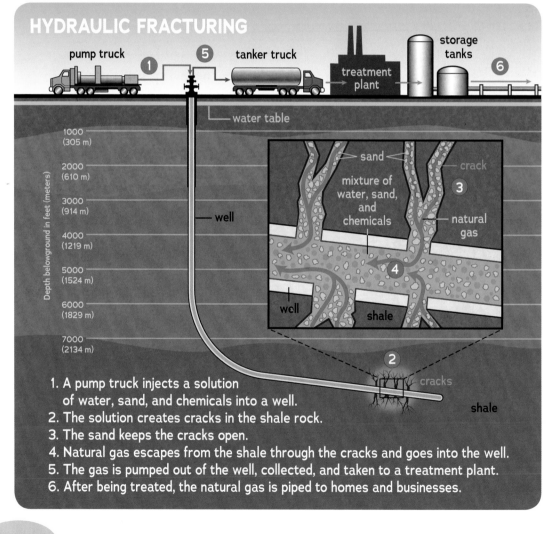

HYDRAULIC FRACTURING

1. A pump truck injects a solution of water, sand, and chemicals into a well.
2. The solution creates cracks in the shale rock.
3. The sand keeps the cracks open.
4. Natural gas escapes from the shale through the cracks and goes into the well.
5. The gas is pumped out of the well, collected, and taken to a treatment plant.
6. After being treated, the natural gas is piped to homes and businesses.

Refining

Most coal is ready to be burned from the time it is mined. But oil and natural gas aren't quite ready to be used straight out of the ground.

Oil and natural gas need to go to a refinery before they can be used as fuel.

Crude oil is refined into gasoline used in cars.

Crude oil is a mixture of many hydrocarbons. Crude oil goes to a refinery. There, machines separate the hydrocarbons. Some of them become gasoline. Others become heating oil or motor oil. Still others are used to make materials such as plastics.

Natural gas also needs some processing. Raw natural gas includes the gases methane, propane, and butane. A natural gas processing plant separates these substances. Then the methane is ready to be piped into homes for heating and cooking. Meanwhile, gases such as butane and propane are also useful fuels.

Natural gas doesn't have a smell, so an odor is added to it as a safety precaution. Natural gas is dangerous if it leaks into a building.

Chapter 3

THE PROS AND CONS OF FOSSIL FUELS

People have been burning fossil fuels for centuries. Fossil fuels are plentiful. They are reliable and easy to use. Advances in science and technology help us find new sources of fossil fuels. They also give us better ways to collect them.

This plant burns coal for energy. What is one advantage of coal and other fossil fuels?

These people speak out against coal-fired power plants.

But fossil fuels may not be a good long-term solution to our energy needs. The debate over their future seems to grow and grow.

Supply

Fossil fuels are a nonrenewable resource. Once they are burned, they are gone. So while Earth still has lots of them, the supply keeps decreasing. We can't just keep burning them forever.

This oil rig has been abandoned because it has pumped up all the oil it can reach.

Many people are looking for alternative energy sources. Renewable resources such as solar power, wind power, and hydropower won't run out as long as the sun shines.

Hydropower uses a river's energy to create electricity.

The Environment

Fossil fuels are hard on the environment. Coal mines scar the ground. Oil spills in the ocean harm and even kill fish, birds, and other sea life. And burning fossil fuels creates a lot of pollution.

This sea otter is covered in oil from a spill. The oil prevents the otter from maintaining its body temperature and can kill it.

Smog is so severe in some cities that people have to wear face masks when they go outside.

Many large cities sit under a haze of smog. The smog is pollution from the gasoline being burned by millions of cars and trucks. Coal-burning power plants also contribute to smog.

Most coal is laced with toxic substances. Some of these harmful substances are released into the atmosphere when coal is burned.

Coal-fired power plants contribute to air pollution.

These protesters are speaking out against fracking because they believe it pollutes water supplies.

Newer collection methods such as fracking can also damage the environment. People are worried that the chemicals used in fracking will seep into water supplies. Fracking has even been found to cause small earthquakes. And the long-term environmental effects of fracking are still unknown.

Climate Change

When fossil fuels are burned, they release lots of carbon dioxide. Scientists warn that releasing a lot of this gas into the atmosphere can cause Earth's climate to change. Global climate change could have terrible effects. Already it is causing ice at the poles to melt and the ocean levels to rise. Climate change could alter weather patterns and disrupt food supplies. And it may even lead to stronger, deadlier storms.

Global climate change is melting the polar ice caps.

Solar panels produce energy only when the sun is up.

But people argue that other energy sources are just not as good. Alternative energy sources aren't as reliable. The wind does not always blow. We can't use the sun's energy at night. But a lump of coal always burns. That's why many people believe fossil fuels will continue to be our best source of energy for a long time.

Chapter 4

THE FUTURE OF FOSSIL FUELS

Fossil fuels aren't going away anytime soon. Alternative energy sources are becoming more popular. But they are not ready to replace fossil fuels altogether. Until they are, coal, oil, and natural gas will remain a key part of the world's energy supply.

Furnaces that burn natural gas heat many homes. What is one drawback of fossil fuels such as natural gas?

But supplies of fossil fuels are dwindling. The fuels aren't as easy to get to as they once were. Deep-sea oil rigs have to drill in deeper, more dangerous waters. As fossil fuels become harder to find, renewable energy will become more and more important.

Deep-sea oil rigs often need to drill in deeper, more dangerous waters to get oil.

Conservation

Using renewable energy is great. But it's not always possible. So we can all help reduce the amount of fossil fuels we use. It's a simple matter of conserving energy.

Biking instead of riding in a car is a good way to reduce fossil fuel use.

How do you do it? There are many ways. Make sure not to leave lights on when you're not in the room. Turn off televisions and computers when you're not using them. Walk to the park instead of getting a ride in the car. Use reusable grocery bags instead of plastic bags. Recycle everything that you can. It takes a lot less energy to recycle materials than it does to make them new. Every little bit helps.

Using reusable grocery bags is just one way you can use less energy.

Glossary

algae: small plants that do not have roots or stems and that grow mainly in water

alternative energy source: a source of energy other than traditional fossil fuels

crude oil: the oil that comes out of the ground and is a mixture of many different hydrocarbons

fossil fuel: a fuel such as coal, natural gas, or oil that was formed over millions of years from the remains of dead plants and animals

hydrocarbon: a compound made of only hydrogen and carbon

nonrenewable: not able to be replenished. Once a nonrenewable form of energy is gone, it is used up for good.

peat: a material composed mainly of decaying plant matter

refine: to remove unwanted elements from a substance

reliable: offering consistently good performance

renewable: able to be replenished over time

shale: a type of rock often rich in oil and natural gas

LERNER

SOURCE

Expand learning beyond the printed book. Download free, complementary educational resources for this book from our website, www.lernersource.com.

Learn More about Coal, Oil, and Natural Gas

Books

Chambers, Catherine. *Energy in Crisis*. New York: Crabtree, 2010. Learn about the energy crisis and concerns about the world's future energy supply. The book also discusses climate change and possible energy solutions for the future.

Fridell, Ron. *Earth-Friendly Energy*. Minneapolis: Lerner Publications, 2009. Explore alternative energy sources, such as hydropower, wind, and solar, and how these energy sources may power our future.

Goodman, Polly. *Understanding Fossil Fuels*. New York: Gareth Stevens, 2011. This title examines the history, the mining, the current use, and the future of fossil fuels.

Hansen, Amy S. *Fossil Fuels: Buried in the Earth*. New York: PowerKids Press, 2010. This title looks at every stage of fossil fuels, from formation through mining and use. Readers will also learn the dangers of fossil fuels and about future alternatives.

Websites

EcoKids—Energy
http://www.ecokids.ca/pub/eco_info/topics/energy/intro/index.cfm
Learn more about energy, how we get it, and how we use it with simple text, quizzes, and games.

Energy Kids—Nonrenewable Energy Sources
http://www.eia.gov/kids/energy.cfm?page=nonrenewable_home-basics
Learn more about coal, oil, and natural gas with pictures, maps, and charts from this website.

How Oil Refining Works
http://science.howstuffworks.com/environmental/energy/oil-refining1
.htm
Take a closer look at the process of refining crude oil into gasoline, heating oil, and many other products.

Index

Photo Acknowledgments

The images in this book are used with the permission of: © iStockphoto.com/caracterdesign, p. 4; © Brad Sauter/Dreamstime.com, p. 5; Iberdrola Renewables, Inc./Department of Energy/National Renewable Energy Laboratory, p. 6; © Publiphoto/Science Source, p. 7; © iStockphoto.com/w-ings, p. 8; © Sam Lund/Independent Picture Service, p. 9; © John R. Kreul/Independent Picture Service, p. 10; © iStockphoto.com/DanBrandenburg, p. 11; © Sumit buranarothtrakul/Shutterstock.com, p. 12; © Velvetweb/Dreamstime.com, p. 13; © Awcnz62/Dreamstime.com, p. 14; © Monty Rakusen/Cultura/Getty Images, p. 15; © iStockphoto.com/westphalia, p. 16; © Bloomberg/Getty Images, p. 17; © Ed Darack/Science Faction/SuperStock, p. 18; © iStockphoto.com/CedarWings, p. 19; © Laura Westlund/Independent Picture Service, p. 20; © iStockphoto.com/RicAguiar, p. 21; © iStockphoto.com/antikainen, p. 22; © Todd Strand/Independent Picture Service, p. 23; © airphoto.gr/Shutterstock.com, p. 24; © Robert Nickelsberg/Getty Images News/Getty Images, p. 25; © Bali58/Dreamstime.com, p. 26; © iStockphoto.com/Jennifer_Sharp, p. 27; © FLPA/SuperStock, p. 28; © iStockphoto.com/sndrk, p. 29; © iStockphoto.com/Schroptschop, p. 30; © a katz/Shutterstock.com, p. 31; © Danita Delimont/Gallo Images/Getty Images, p. 32; © iStockphoto.com/RyanKing999, p. 33; © iStockphoto.com/nycshooter, p. 34; © iStockphoto.com/landbysea, p. 35; © Brian Summers/First Light/Getty Images, p. 36; © Fuse/Thinkstock, p. 37.

Front cover: © RonFullHD/Shutterstock.com.

Main body text set in Adrianna Regular 14/20
Typeface provided by Chank